LEARN TO DRAW...
CARS, TRUCKS, and TRAINS!

Illustrated and designed by
Kerren Barbas Steckler

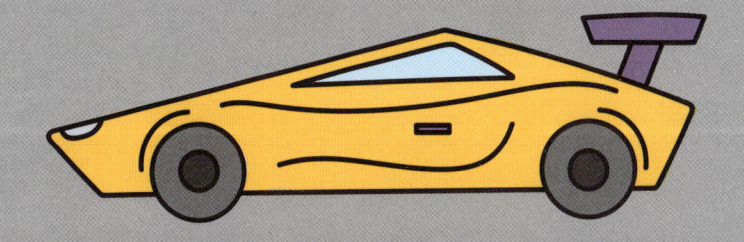
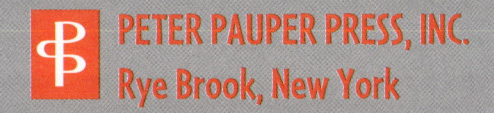

PETER PAUPER PRESS, INC.
Rye Brook, New York

PETER PAUPER PRESS

In 1928, at the age of twenty-two, Peter Beilenson began printing books on a small press in the basement of his parents' home in Larchmont, New York. Peter—and later, his wife, Edna—sought to create fine books that sold at "prices even a pauper could afford."

Today, still family owned and operated, Peter Pauper Press continues to honor our founders' legacy of quality, value, and fun for big kids and small kids alike.

Copyright © 2025 Peter Pauper Press, Inc.
3 International Drive
Rye Brook, NY 10573 USA

Published in the United Kingdom and Europe by
Peter Pauper Press, Inc.
Units 2-3 Spring Business Park
Stanbridge Road
Havant, Hampshire PO9 2GJ, UK

Visit us at www.peterpauper.com

Are you ready to
learn how to draw
over 40 cool things that go?

Hey, young
artists!

It's easy and fun!
Just follow these steps:

First, pick a car, truck, or train you want to draw.

Next, trace over the picture with a pencil. This will give you a feel for how to draw the lines.

Then, following the numbers, start drawing each new step (shown in red) of the picture in the empty space in each scene, or on a piece of paper. Some pictures will have you start out by drawing some basic shapes to use as guidelines. When you are finished with your drawing, erase these gray lines.

Lastly, if you're an awesome artist (and of course, you are!), try drawing a whole scene with one or more vehicles. And remember, don't worry if your drawings look different from the ones in this book—there are all sorts of cars, trucks, and trains in the world!

You're on your way to creating your own masterpieces on the move!

GET READY! GET SET! DRAW!

DOUBLE DECKER BUS

1.

START by drawing
this simple shape.

2.

THEN, follow each new step in red.

3.

ERASE the gray lines.

4.

5.

6.

POLICE CAR

1.

START by drawing
this simple shape.

2.

THEN, follow each new step in red.

3.

4.

5.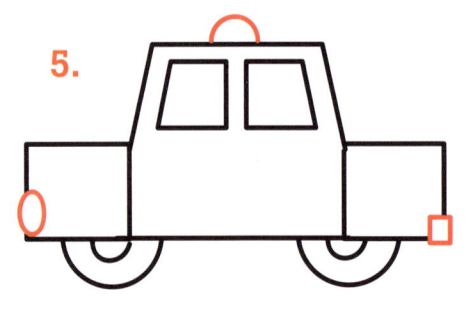

6.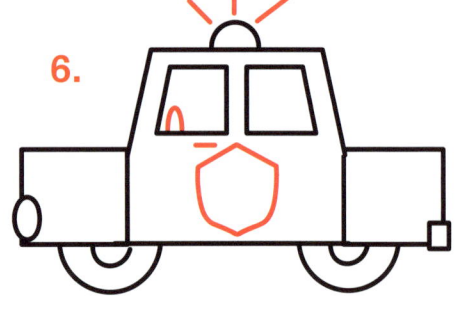

Trace over us for practice!

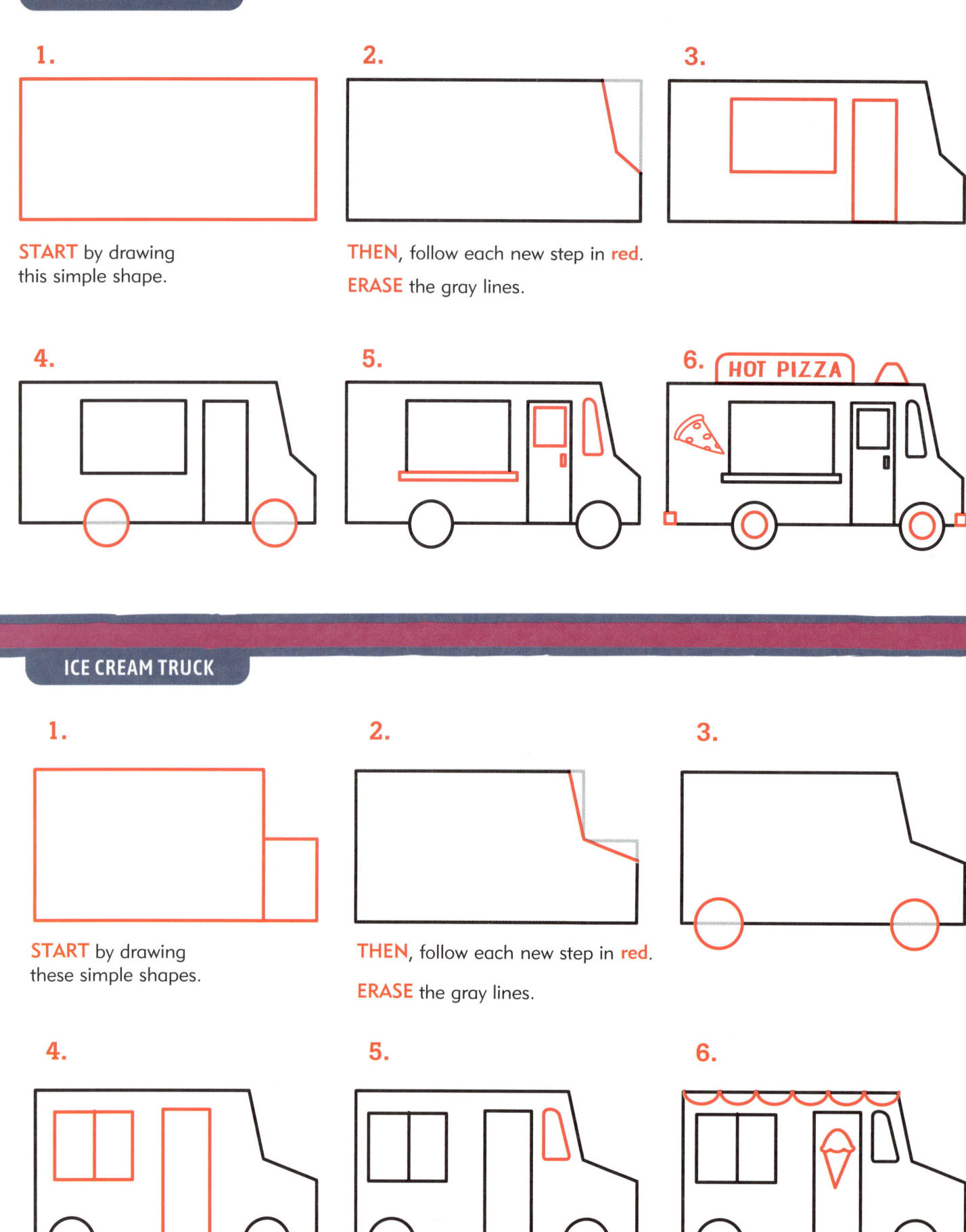

FOOD TRUCK

1.

START by drawing this simple shape.

2.

THEN, follow each new step in red.

ERASE the gray lines.

3.

4.

5.

6. HOT PIZZA

ICE CREAM TRUCK

1.

START by drawing these simple shapes.

2.

THEN, follow each new step in red.

ERASE the gray lines.

3.

4.

5.

6.

TAXI

1. START by drawing these simple shapes.

2. THEN, follow each new step in red.
ERASE the gray lines.

3.

4.

5.

6.

AMBULANCE

1. START by drawing this simple shape.

2. THEN, follow each new step in red.

3. ERASE the gray lines.

4.

5.

6.

SCHOOL BUS

1. START by drawing these simple shapes.

2. THEN, follow each new step in red. ERASE the gray lines.

3.

4.

5.

6.

FIRE TRUCK

1. START by drawing these simple shapes.

2. THEN, follow each new step in red.

3.

4.

5.

6.

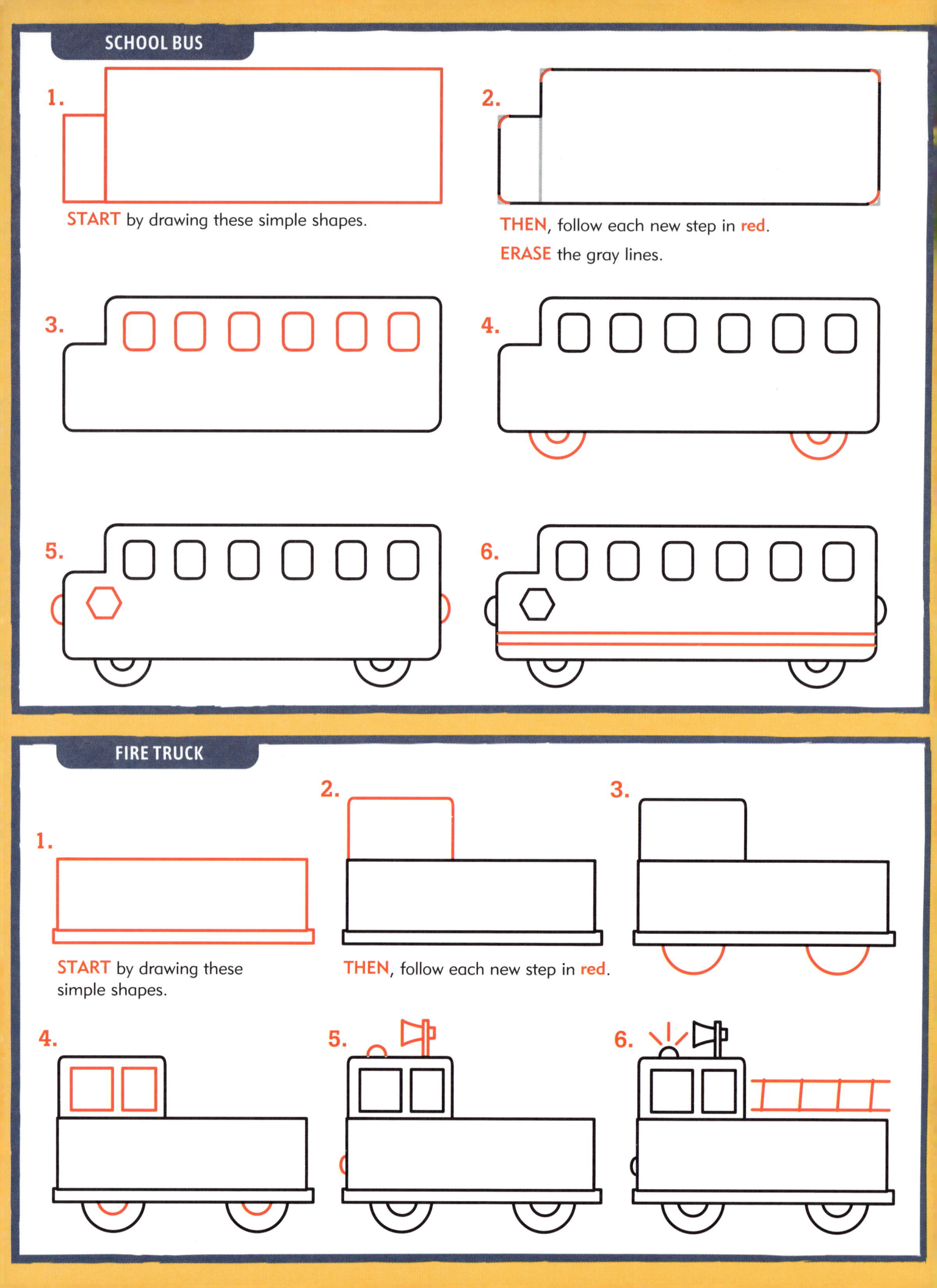

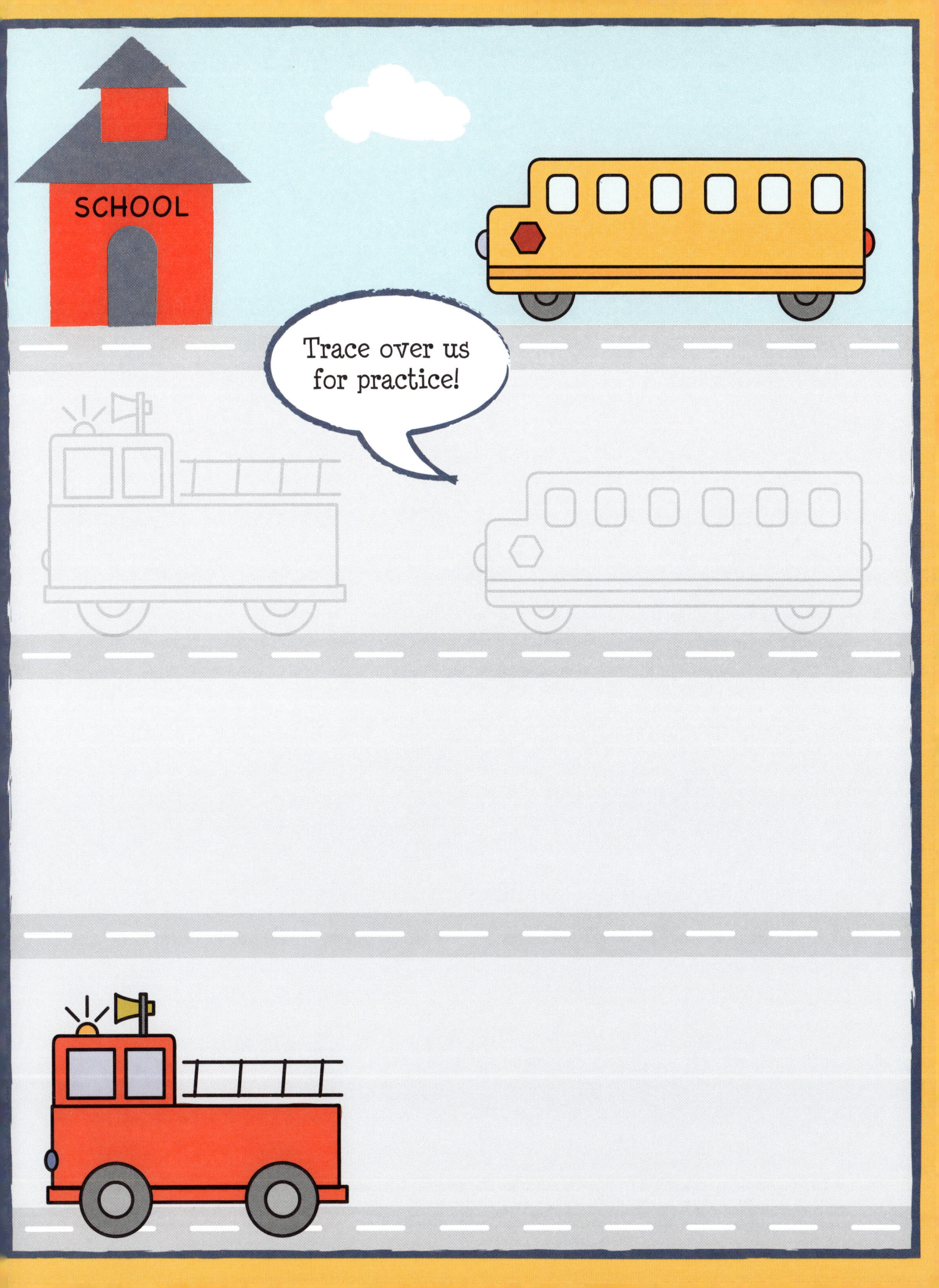

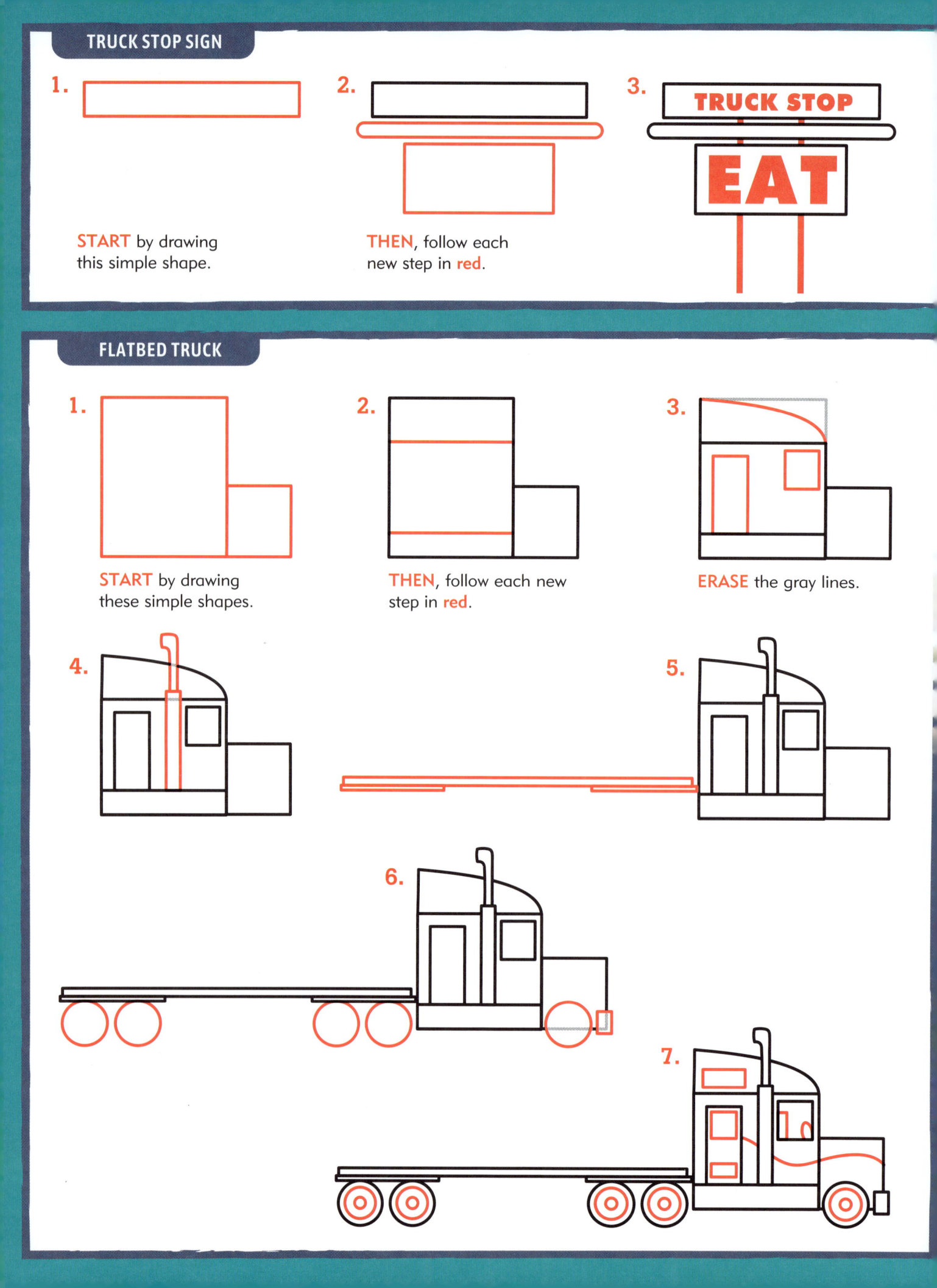

TRUCK STOP SIGN

1.

START by drawing this simple shape.

2.

THEN, follow each new step in **red**.

3.

TRUCK STOP

EAT

FLATBED TRUCK

1.

START by drawing these simple shapes.

2.

THEN, follow each new step in **red**.

3.

ERASE the gray lines.

4.

5.

6.

7.

TRUCK STOP

EAT

Trace over us for practice!

BIG RIG

1.

START by drawing this simple shape.

2.

THEN, follow each new step in red.

3.

4.

DUMP TRUCK

1.

START by drawing these simple shapes.

2.

THEN, follow each new step in red.

ERASE the gray lines.

3.

4.

5.

6.

Trace over us
for practice!

1.

START by drawing these simple shapes.

2.

THEN, follow each new step in red.

3.

4.

1.

START by drawing this simple shape.

2.

THEN, follow each new step in red.

ERASE the gray lines.

3.

4.

5.

6.

Trace over us for practice!

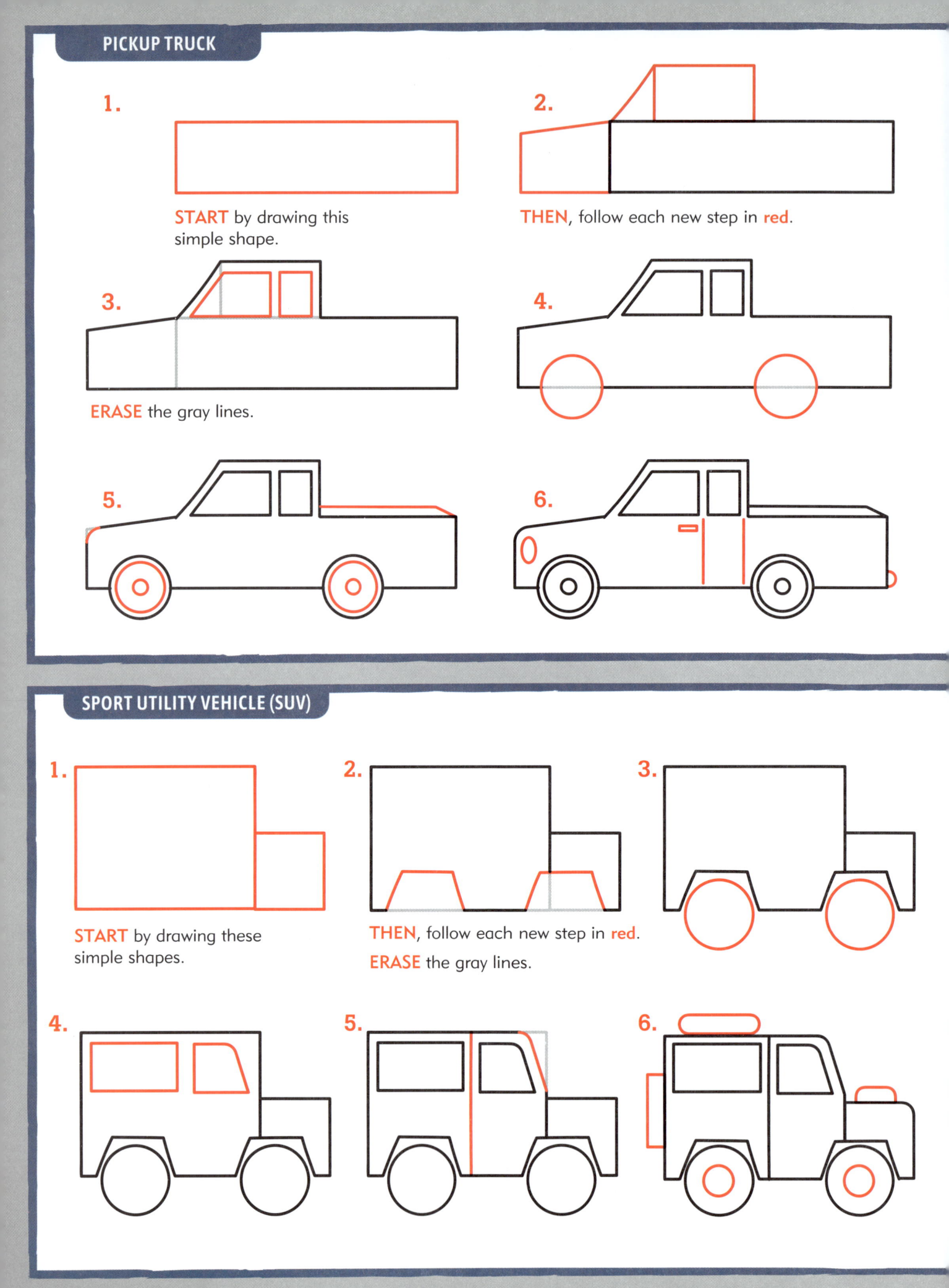

PICKUP TRUCK

1. START by drawing this simple shape.

2. THEN, follow each new step in red.

3. ERASE the gray lines.

4.

5.

6.

SPORT UTILITY VEHICLE (SUV)

1. START by drawing these simple shapes.

2. THEN, follow each new step in red. ERASE the gray lines.

3.

4.

5.

6.

Trace over us for practice!

1.

START by drawing this simple shape.

2.

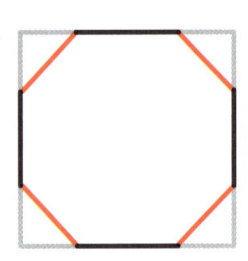

THEN, follow each new step in **red**.

ERASE the gray lines.

3.

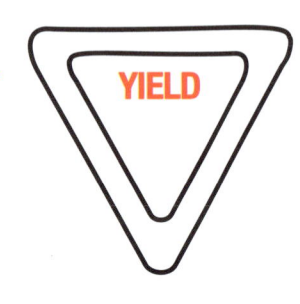

1.

START by drawing this simple shape.

2.

THEN, follow each new step in **red**.

3.

1.

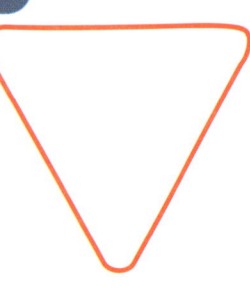

START by drawing this simple shape.

2.

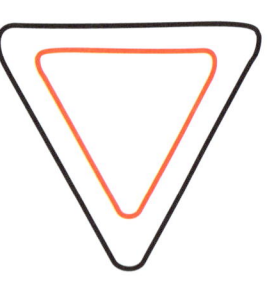

THEN, follow each new step in **red**.

3.

YIELD

1. **2.**

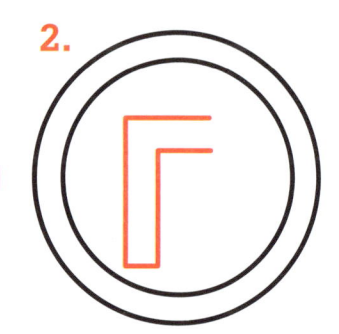

START by drawing these simple shapes.

THEN, follow each new step in **red**.

3. **4.**

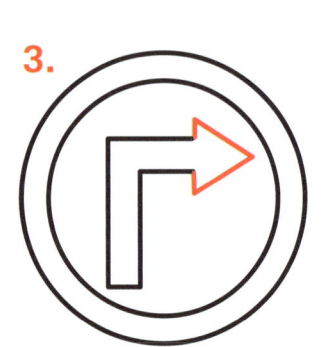 

ERASE the gray lines.

Trace over us for practice!

STOP

GOLF CART

1.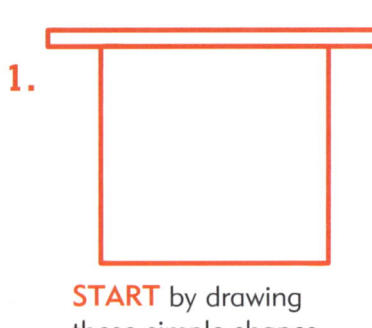

START by drawing these simple shapes.

2.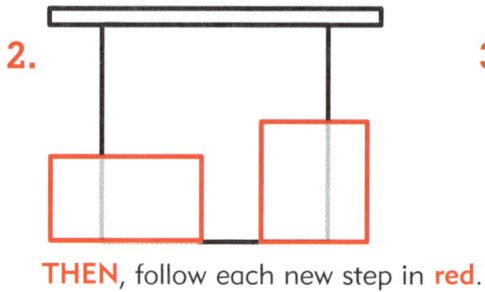

THEN, follow each new step in red.

ERASE the gray lines.

3.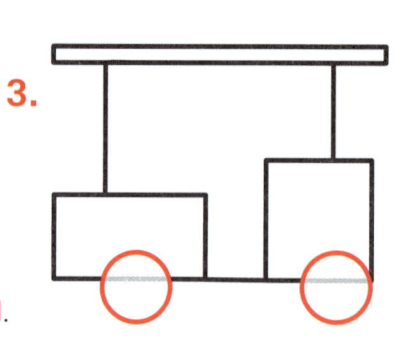

4.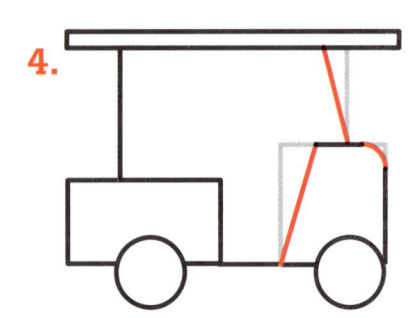

5.

6.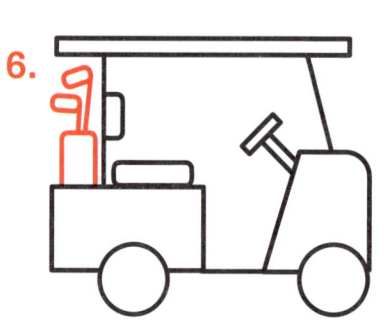

CONVERTIBLE

1.

START by drawing this simple shape.

2.

THEN, follow each new step in red.

ERASE the gray lines.

3.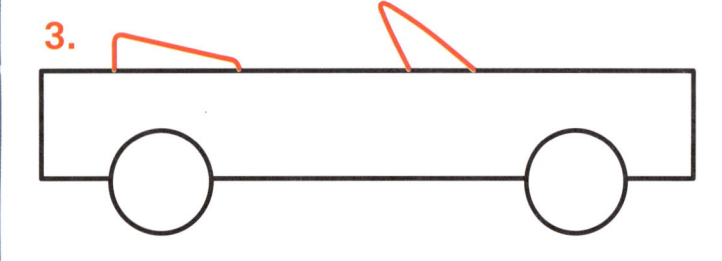

4.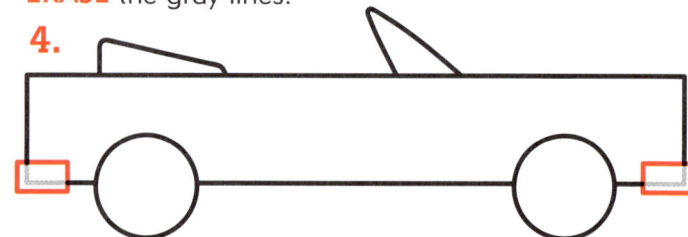

5.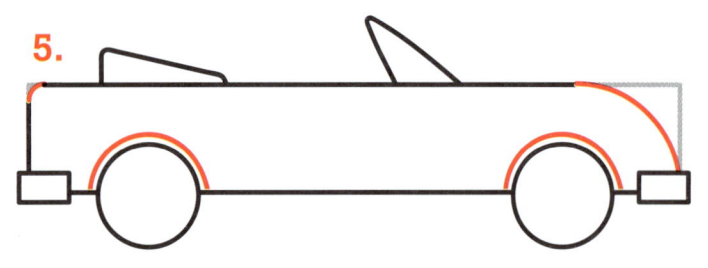

6.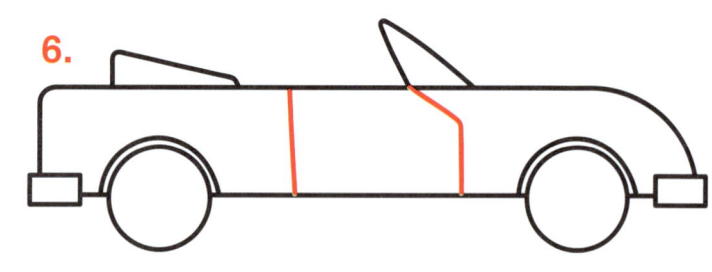

7.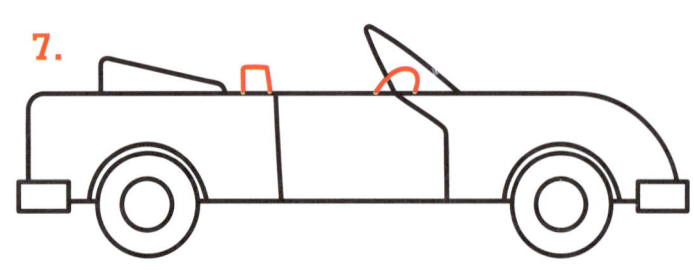

8.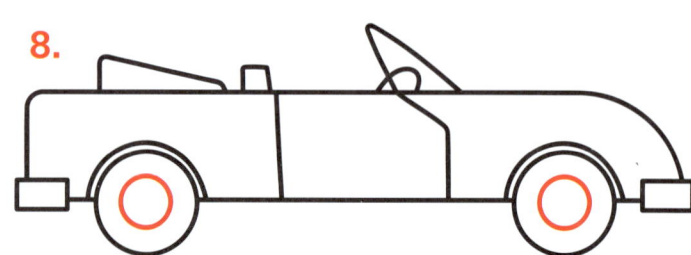

TRAIN ENGINE

1.

START by drawing this simple shape.

2.

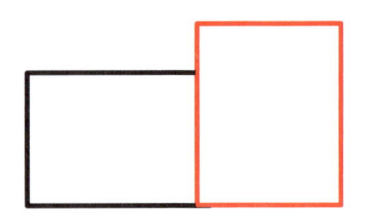

THEN, follow each new step in red.

3.

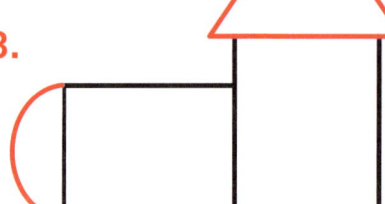

4.

5.

6.

CABOOSE

1.

START by drawing these simple shapes.

2.

THEN, follow each new step in red.

ERASE the gray lines.

3.

4.

TROLLEY

1.

START by drawing these simple shapes.

2.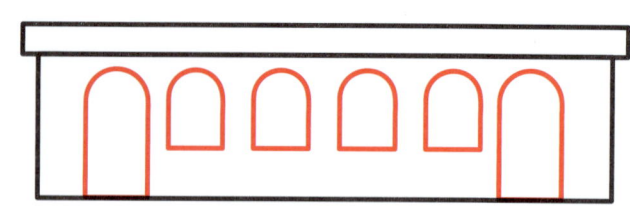

THEN, follow each new step in red.

3.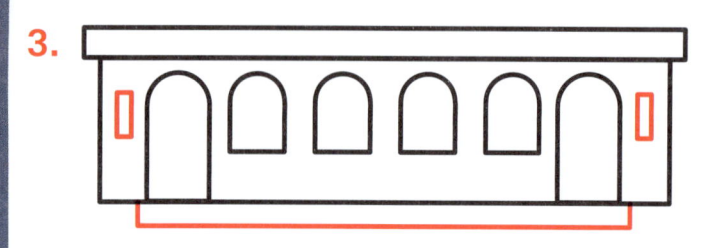

4.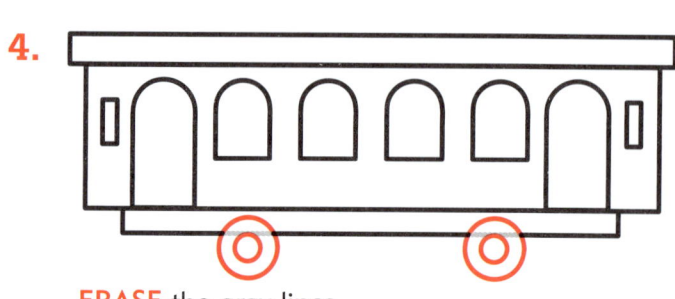

ERASE the gray lines.

5.

6.

CLASSIC CAR

1.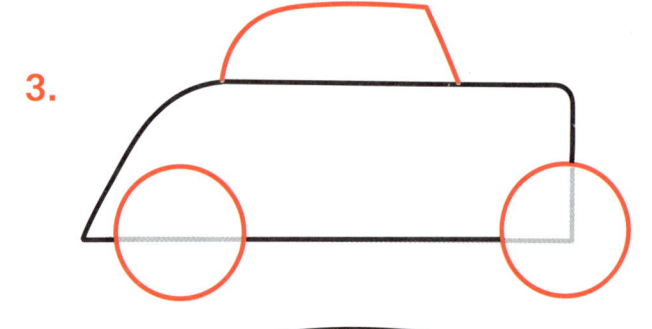

START by drawing this simple shape.

2.

THEN, follow each new step in red.
ERASE the gray lines.

3.

4.

5.

6.

MINIVAN

1.

START by drawing this simple shape.

2.

THEN, follow each new step in red.

3.

ERASE the gray lines.

4.

5.

6.

BUGGY

1.

START by drawing this simple shape.

2.

THEN, follow each new step in red.
ERASE the gray lines.

3.

4.

5.

6.

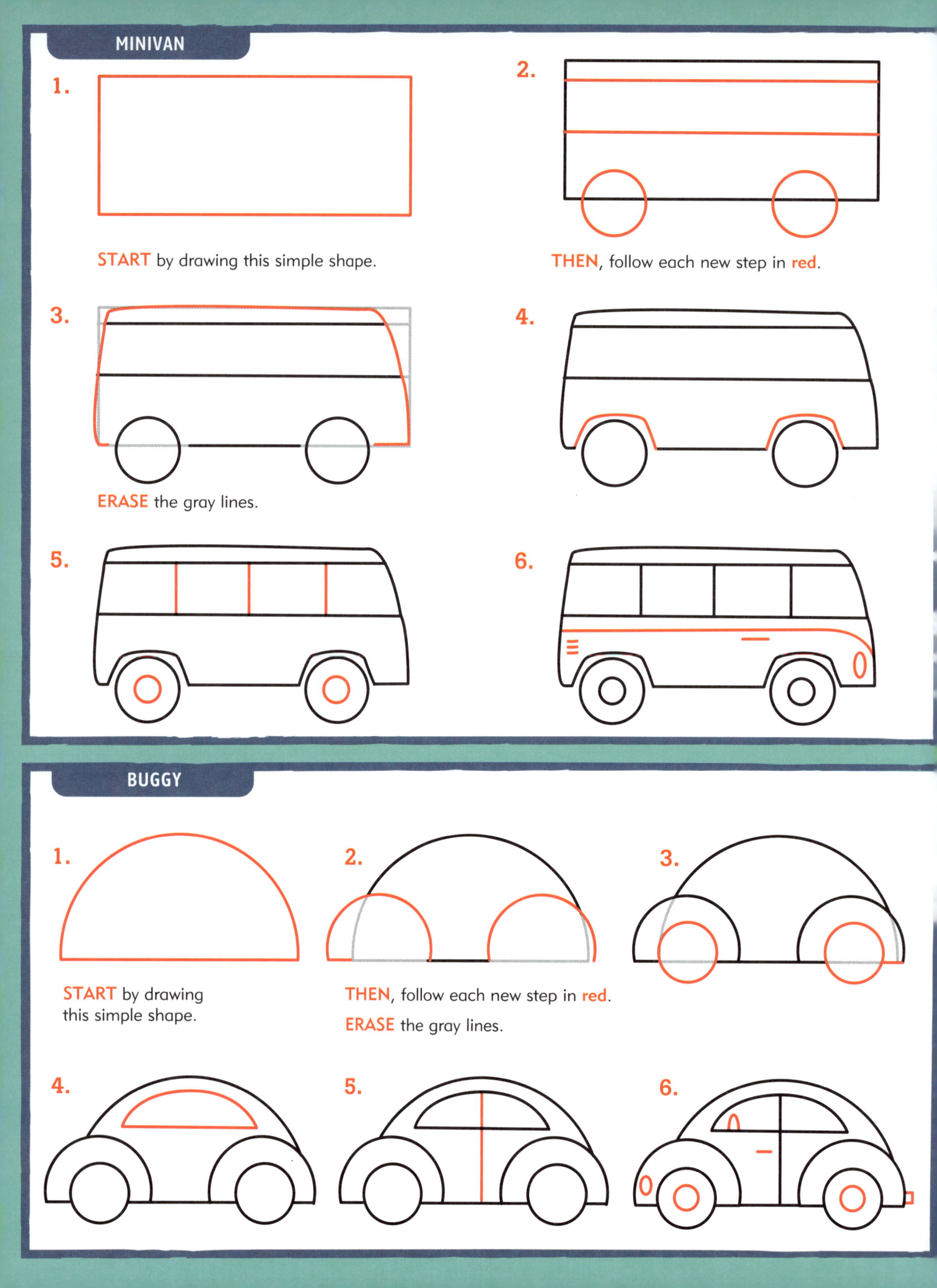

MAIL TRUCK

1.

START by drawing this simple shape.

2.

THEN, follow each new step in red.

3.

ERASE the gray lines.

4.

5.

6.

GARBAGE TRUCK

1.

START by drawing these simple shapes.

2.

THEN, follow each new step in red.

ERASE the gray lines.

3.

4.

Trace over us for practice!

TRAIN

1. START by drawing this simple shape.

2. THEN, follow each new step.

3.

4.

5. ERASE the gray lines.

6.

SUBWAY

1. START by drawing this simple shape.

2. THEN, follow each new step in red. ERASE the gray lines.

3.

4.

5.

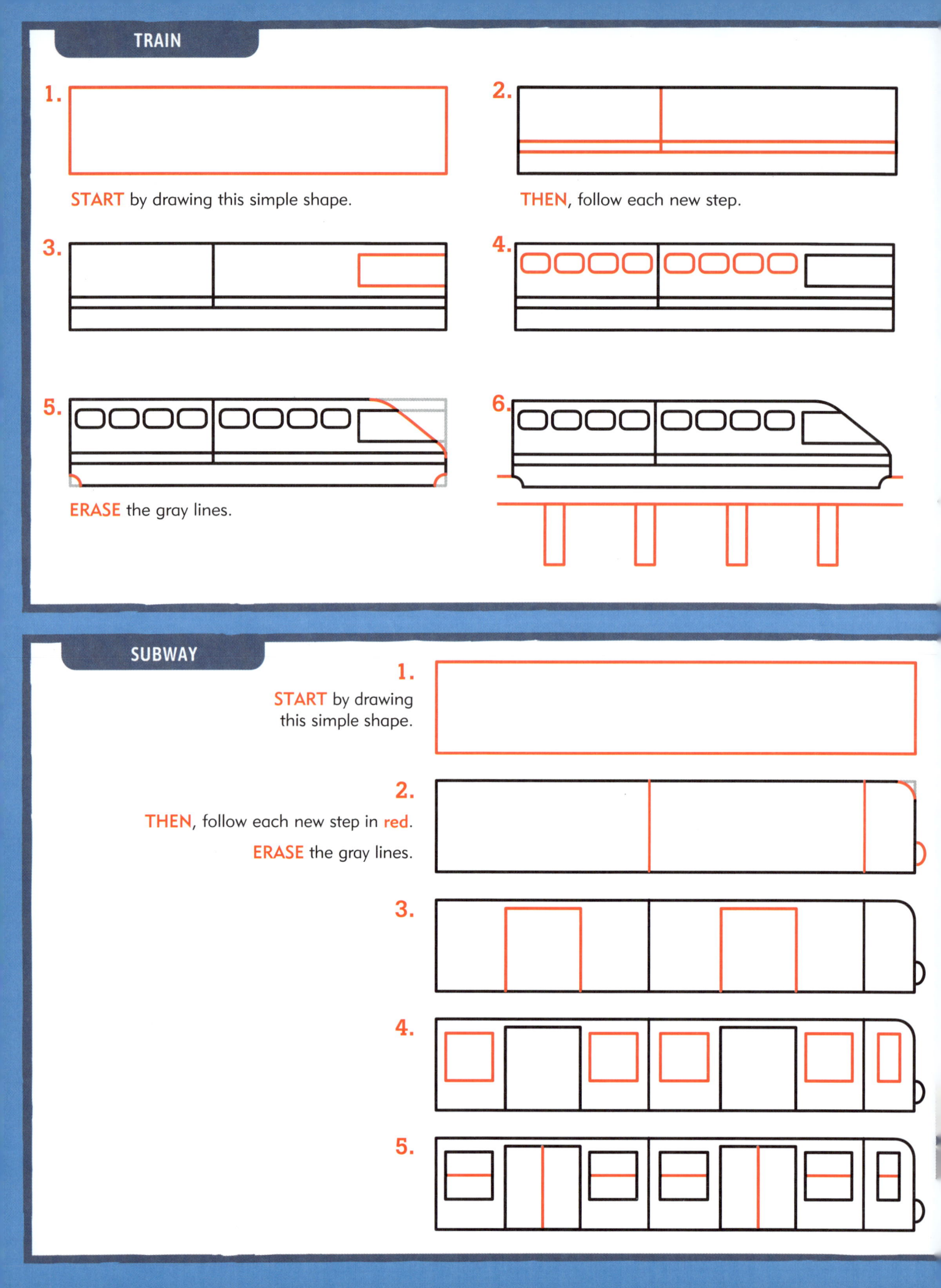

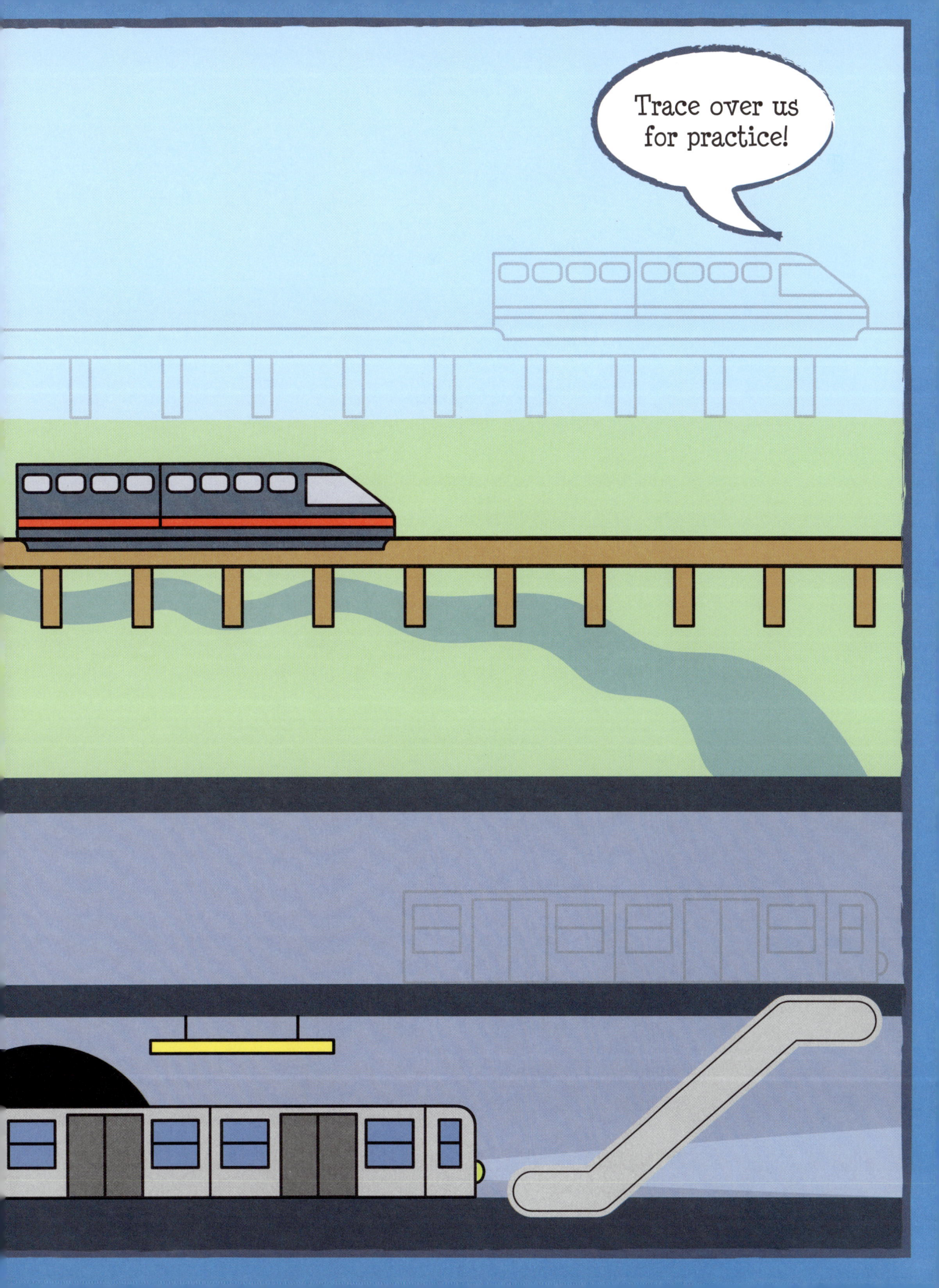

ATV

1.

START by drawing
this simple shape.

2.

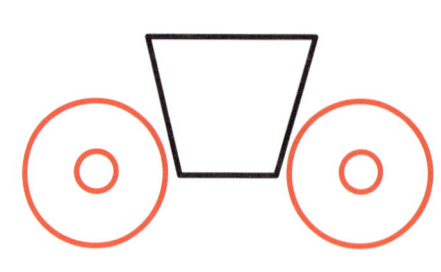

THEN, follow each new
step in red.

3.

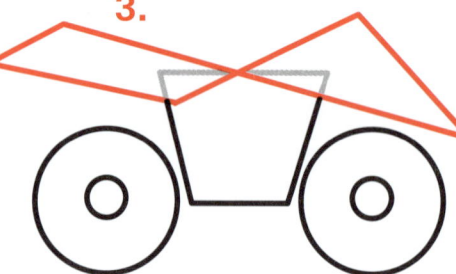

ERASE the gray lines.

4.

5.

6.

RIDING MOWER

1.

START by drawing
this simple shape.

2.

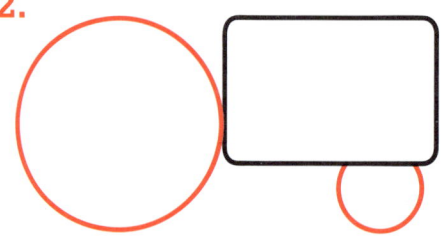

THEN, follow each new
step in red.

3.

4.

5.

6.

BACKHOE

1.

START by drawing this simple shape.

2.

THEN, follow each new step in red.

3.

ERASE the gray lines.

4.

5.

6.

EXCAVATOR

1.

START by drawing these simple shapes.

2.

THEN, follow each new step in red.

ERASE the gray lines.

3.

4.

5.

6.

7.

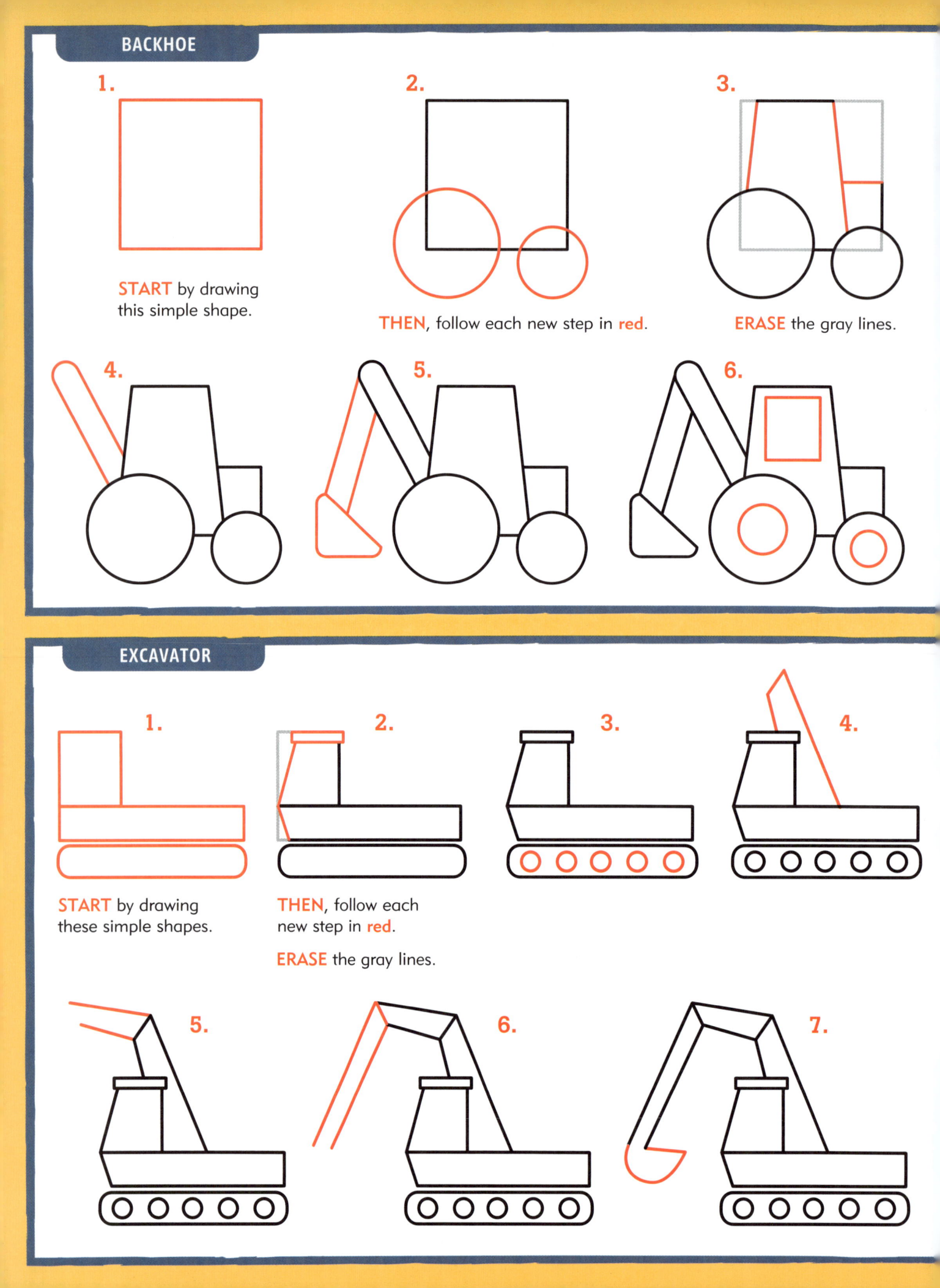

Trace over us for practice!

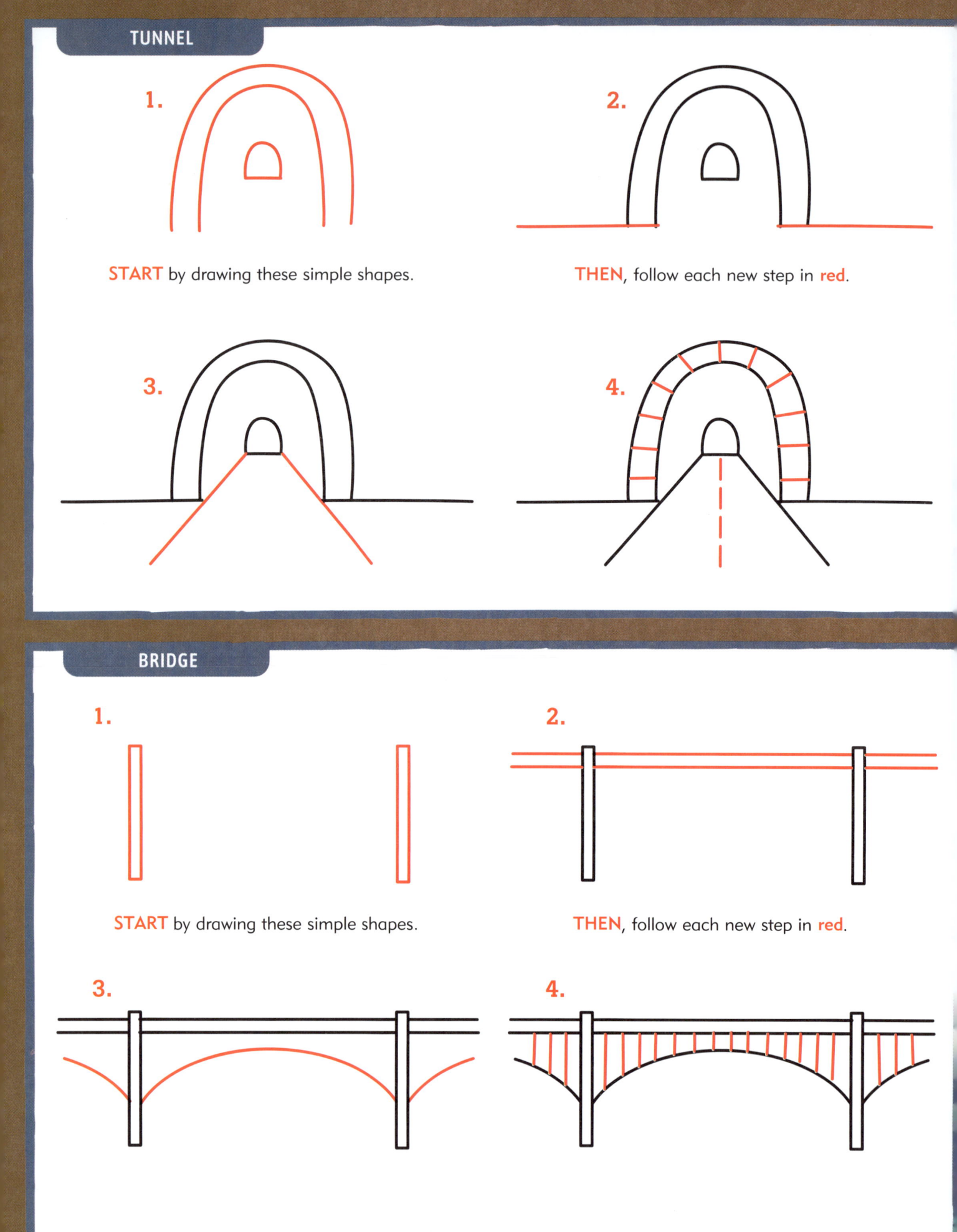

TUNNEL

1. START by drawing these simple shapes.

2. THEN, follow each new step in red.

3.

4.

BRIDGE

1. START by drawing these simple shapes.

2. THEN, follow each new step in red.

3.

4.

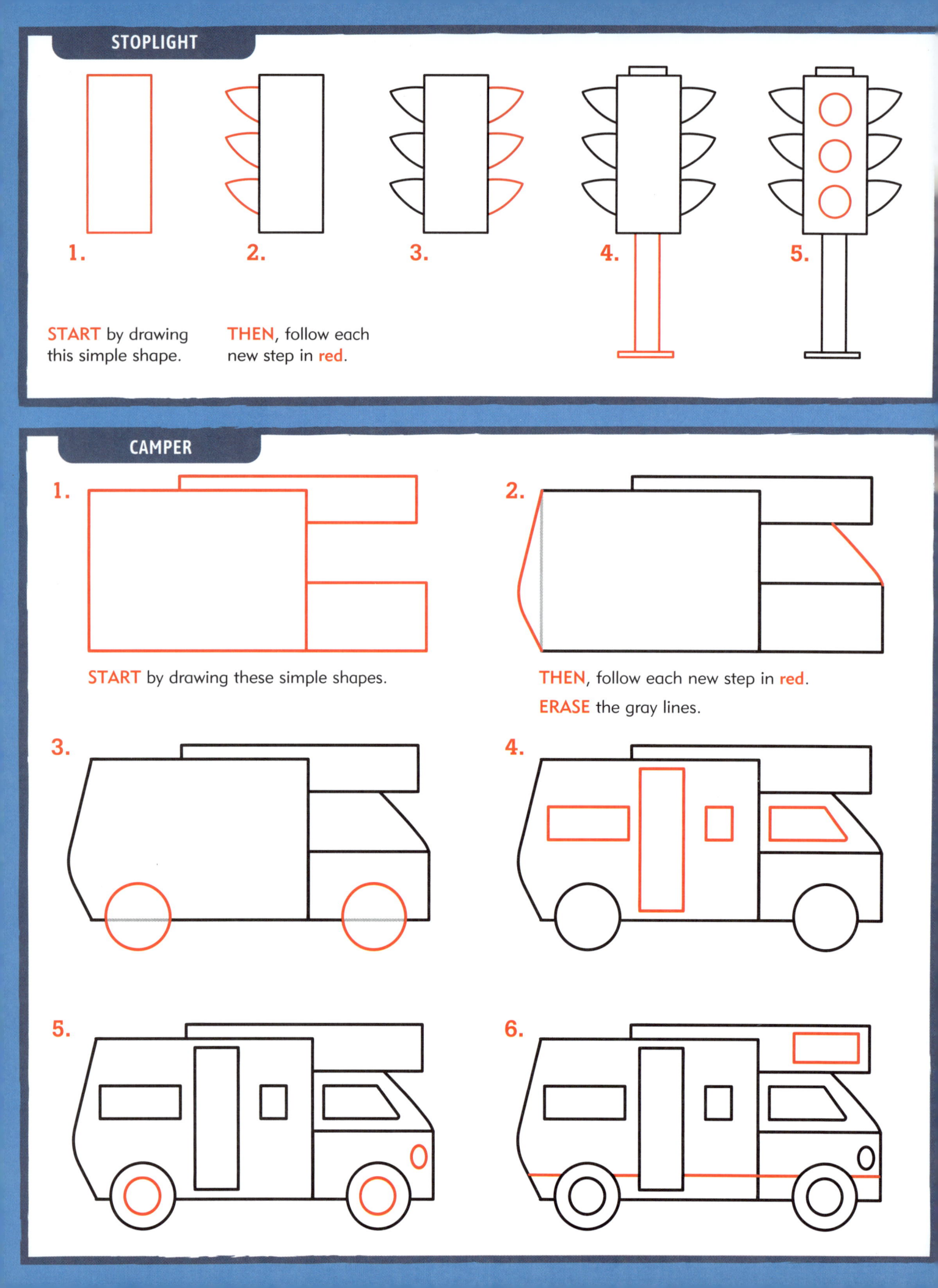

STOPLIGHT

1.

2.

3.

4.

5.

START by drawing this simple shape.

THEN, follow each new step in red.

CAMPER

1.

START by drawing these simple shapes.

2.

THEN, follow each new step in red.
ERASE the gray lines.

3.

4.

5.

6.

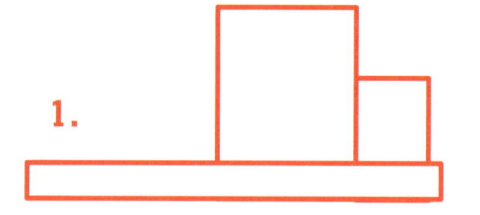

1.

START by drawing
these simple shapes.

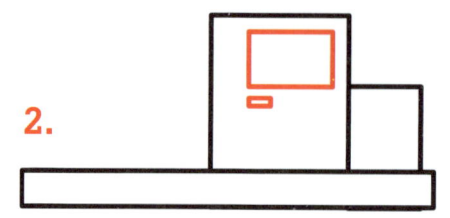

2.

THEN, follow each new
step in red.

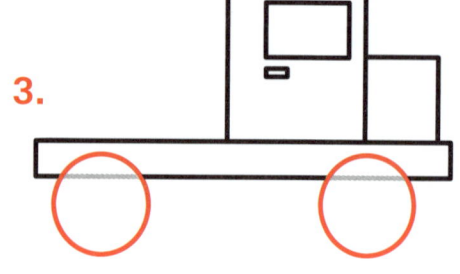

3.

ERASE the gray lines.

4.

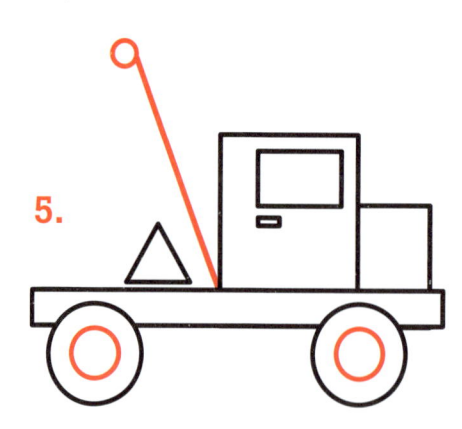

5.

6.

CEMENT MIXER

1.

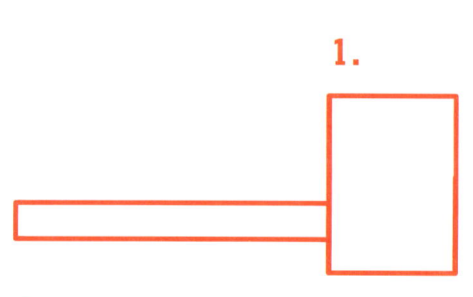

START by drawing
these simple shapes.

2.

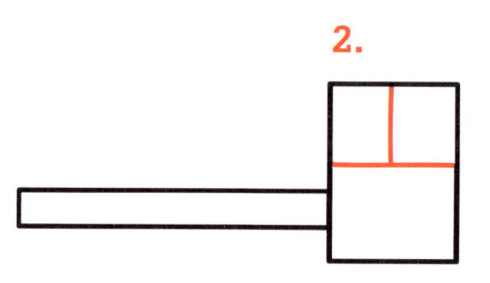

THEN, follow each new
step in red.

3.

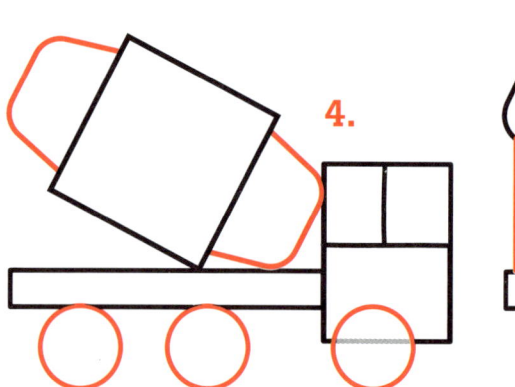

4.

ERASE the gray lines.

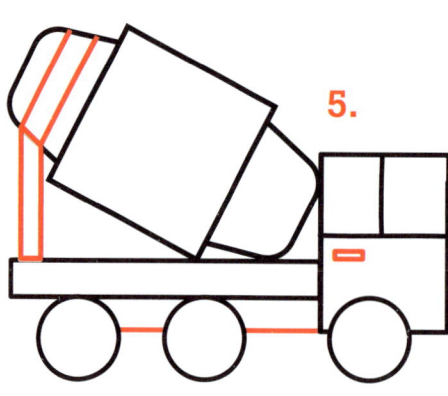

5.

6.

Trace over us for practice!

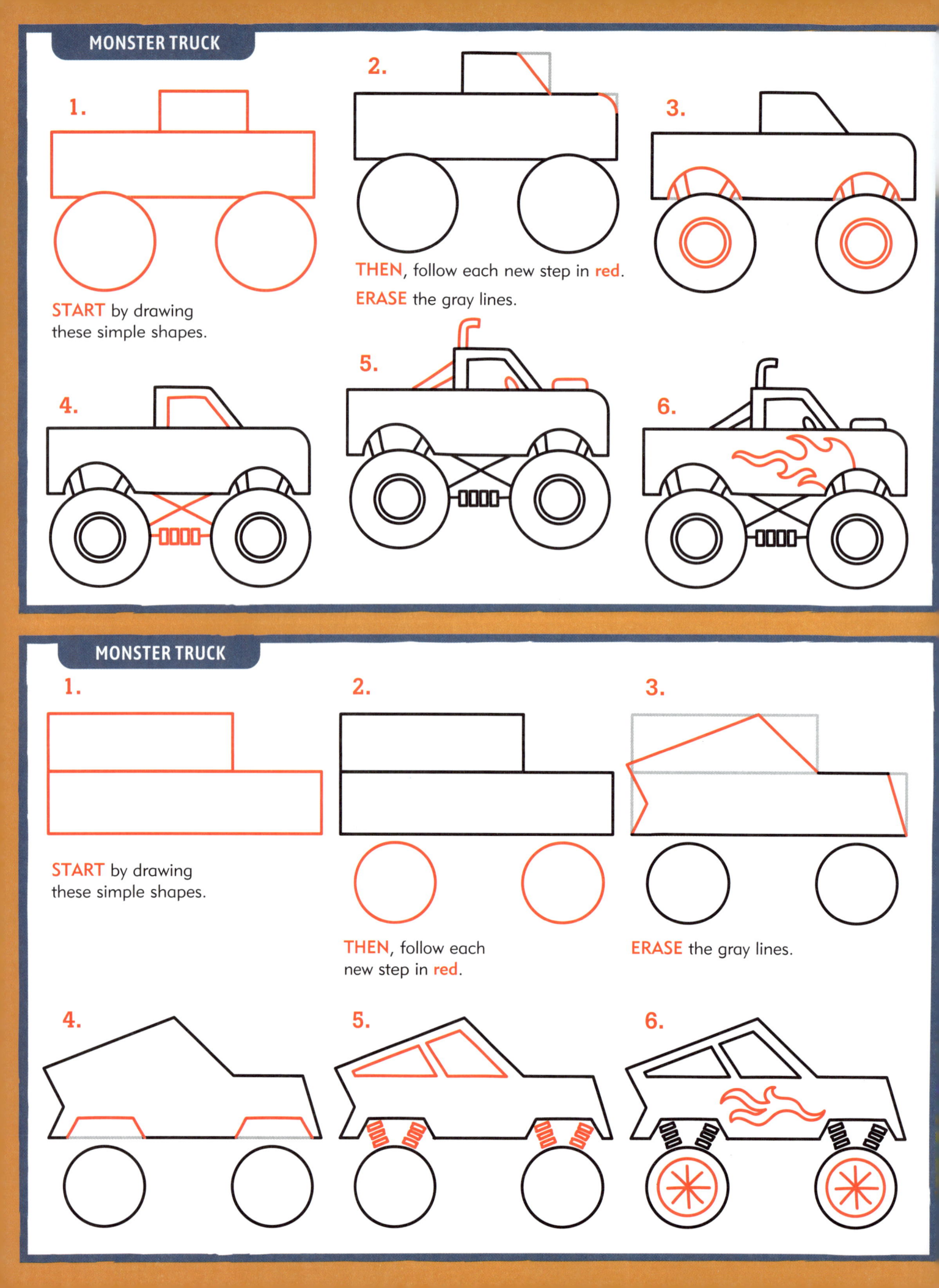

MONSTER TRUCK

1. START by drawing these simple shapes.

2. THEN, follow each new step in red. ERASE the gray lines.

3.

4.

5.

6.

MONSTER TRUCK

1. START by drawing these simple shapes.

2. THEN, follow each new step in red.

3. ERASE the gray lines.

4.

5.

6.

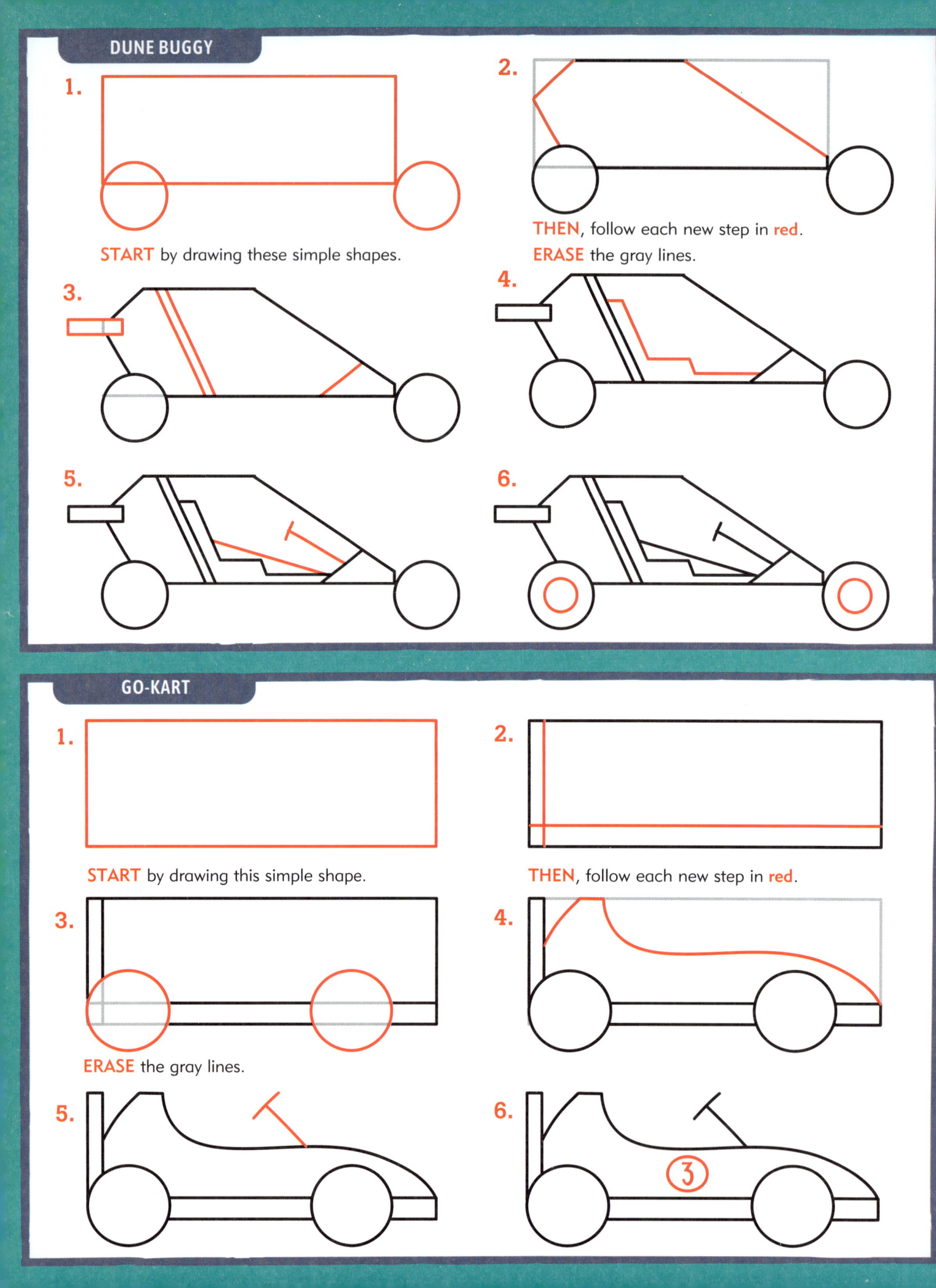

DUNE BUGGY

1. START by drawing these simple shapes.

2. THEN, follow each new step in red. ERASE the gray lines.

3.

4.

5.

6.

GO-KART

1. START by drawing this simple shape.

2. THEN, follow each new step in red.

3. ERASE the gray lines.

4.

5.

6.

We've reached the end
and now we're done.
Drawing cars, trucks, and trains
is so much fun!